MAKE THE
CHANGE

LIVING THE LIFE OF YOUR DREAMS

IMAOBONG ODUTOLA, MD

authorHOUSE®

AuthorHouse™
1663 Liberty Drive
Bloomington, IN 47403
www.authorhouse.com
Phone: 833-262-8899

Published by AuthorHouse 08/31/2020

ISBN: 978-1-7283-7147-4 (sc)
ISBN: 978-1-7283-7146-7 (hc)
ISBN: 978-1-7283-7145-0 (e)

Library of Congress Control Number: 2020916148

Print information available on the last page.

This book is printed on acid-free paper.

Scripture taken from The Holy Bible, King James Version.

DEDICATION

To the Holy Spirit - My Father, who dwells in me, for being an ever present help, for giving my life a purposeful meaning, for making my dreams come true, for believing in me and for the demonstration of His Spirit and Power.

To my beloved husband, for being a constant support; giving his attention, listening ears, patience, and contributions to this dream turned reality. Thank you for believing in me and in the vision, God has placed in my heart.

To my lovely children, for their unparalleled support of whom I drew inspirations regularly from by their calm, gentle and loving dispositions.

CONTENTS

Introduction

If you change things in the realm of the spirit, nothing will stop them from being changed here on the earth, because the spiritual controls the physical. Many people all around the world are caught in the web of pains, depression, confusion, lack, sickness, weakness, poverty etc. Many have not known how to get out of situations that they find themselves. Some are oblivious of the greater one who lives in them in other that they might enjoy the beautiful life He gave to them.

Sadly, most people die in their precarious state and devastation when they could have lived longer if they had knowledge of God's word to change their dire situations.

How can a man live a life of peace with prosperity, perfect health and strength, being fruitful and productive in every endeavour especially in today's world where the order of the day is terrorism, wickedness, all manner of infections, pandemics, and evil trailing the news and filling the hearts of men with fear rather than faith?

Is it possible for one to live a successful life of victory and at every count? Some will even argue that there is no such thing as a successful life with everyday challenges but it might interest you to know that the life of victory, glory, success, health and fulfilment is possible in Christ; because that's exactly the kind of life He gave to us and the reason why He came. He came that we may have life and that we may live that life to the full, till it overflows (John 10:10 AMPC).

What the devil does is to kill, steal and destroy the joy, health, and love in Man's heart and try to prevent man from living the victorious life in Christ.

The life of victory and glory is for us. That successful life of progress where you move in the upward and forward direction only is possible when you choose to make a turn from the past to a new direction in Christ. Learn how to move from poverty to success, from being a victim to a victor, from lack to abundance, from fear to courage, from disappointment to joy.

In Jesus dwells the fulness of the God head bodily and He takes His abode in you from the day you were saved. If it be so, that Jesus lives in you through the Holy Spirit, then it therefore means that you can be anything you want to be and you can change any circumstance you face to your favour. However, many are yet to realise this truth and those who may have realised it are yet to put the word of God to work in their lives.

If that same Spirit that raised Jesus from the dead lives inside you, He that raised up Jesus from the dead shall also quicken your mortal body (Romans 8:11). So why are people still sick, diseased, and infirmed? If the scripture is actually true that it was the same Spirit that raised Jesus that lives in them (which of course the scripture is true), then anyone who is sick in his or her body should be able to take God's word for what it says and also put His word to work in other to live in divine health.

Some believe that God's word can change their situations yet have no knowledge as to how to apply the word and appropriate the desired change. What do I have to do to see a change in my situation? How can

I make a lasting change? How long do I have to wait to see a change? When can I make changes in life?

There are several people in the scriptures that were in dire situations and needed a change of which we will study about in this book. Let us see how they took advantage of God's word to make changes in their lives.

Chapter 1

DESIRE FOR A CHANGE

A desire for a change is not a desire if it is not strong and compelling

The book of Esther tells an inspiring story of a young lady who experienced God's favour and faithfulness.

Let us look at Esther 1:10-12:

On the seventh day, when the heart of the king was merry with wine, he commanded Mehuman, Biztha, Harbona, Bigtha, and Abagtha, Zethar, and Carcas, the seven chamberlains that served in the presence of Ahasuerus the king,

To bring Vashti the queen before the king with the crown royal, to shew the people and the princes her beauty: for she was fair to look on.

But the queen Vashti refused to come at the king's commandment by His chamberlains: therefore, was the king very wroth, and His anger burned in Him.

Now the disobedience of Queen Vashti made the king and his princes issue a decree against Vashti that she should not present herself before the king and that her royal estate should be given to a woman deemed more deserving. Hence the king's servants sought for young fair virgins in Shushan, and any of the maidens who pleased the king would be queen instead of Vashti.

When Mordecai heard of the decree, he took Esther, his uncle's daughter to the king's palace where Haggai was. Many other young women also showed up at Shushan, the citadel, to be placed under the custody of Haggai. The bible records that Esther found favour before Haggai the custodian and he gave her beauty preparations besides her allowance and kept her and her maid servants in the best place.

When it was Esther's turn to go before the king, she requested nothing but what Haggai the king's eunuch advised, and she obtained favour in the sight of all who saw her. Hence Esther was taken to King Ahasuerus and He loved her more than all the other women and she obtained favour in his sight, so the king set the royal crown upon her head instead of Vashti (Esther 2:15-17).

To the surprise of many, Esther became queen. She enjoyed the pleasures of the palace as expected, and the rights and privileges of being the Queen of Ahasuerus, having servants at her beck and call. Life surely was sweet and wonderful for Esther with such an exalted position, and no one would have thought there would be trouble in the land to demand Esther's attention until Haman conspired against the Jews. Now everyone was "up on their toes" because trouble had set in.

Let us look at Esther 3:1-6:

> *After these things did king Ahasuerus promote Haman the son of Hammedatha the Agagite, and advanced him, and set his seat above all the princes that were with him.*
>
> *And all the king's servants, that were in the king's gate, bowed, and reverenced Haman: for the king had so commanded concerning him. But Mordecai bowed not, nor did him reverence.*
>
> *Then the king's servants, which were in the king's gate, said unto Mordecai, Why transgressest thou the king's commandment?*
>
> *Now it came to pass, when they spake daily unto him, and he hearkened not unto them, that they told Haman, to see whether Mordecai's matters would stand: for he had told them that he was a Jew.*
>
> *And when Haman saw that Mordecai bowed not, nor did him reverence, then was Haman full of wrath.*
>
> *And he thought scorn to lay hands on Mordecai alone; for they had shewed him the people of Mordecai: wherefore Haman sought to destroy all the Jews that were throughout the whole kingdom of Ahasuerus, even the people of Mordecai.*

There is more to this story in Esther 3:8-11,13:

> *And Haman said unto king Ahasuerus, there is a certain people scattered abroad and dispersed among the people in all the provinces of thy kingdom; and their laws are diverse from all people; neither keep they the king's laws: therefore it is not for the king's profit to suffer them.*

> *If it please the king, let it be written that they may be destroyed: and I will pay ten thousand talents of silver to the hands of those that have the charge of the business, to bring it into the king's treasuries.*

> *And the king took his ring from his hand and gave it unto Haman the son of Hammedatha the Agagite, the Jews' enemy.*

> *And the king said unto Haman, the silver is given to thee, the people also, to do with them as it seemeth good to thee....*

> *And the letters were sent by posts into all the king's provinces, to destroy, to kill, and to cause to perish, all Jews, both young and old, little children and women, in one day, even upon the thirteenth day of the twelfth month, which is the month Adar, and to take the spoil of them for a prey.*

With this kind of decree against the Jews, there was certainly perplexity in the city as a result. When Mordecai heard about all that transpired against them, he tore his clothes and put on sackcloth and ashes, and the Bible says he cried out with a loud and bitter cry. There was great mourning among the Jews with fasting, weeping and wailing, and many lay in sackcloth and ashes (Esther 4: 1-3).

There was panic everywhere, and fear creeped in; fear of death sparing no Jews, not even their little ones. They would have thought no one could escape this. I can imagine mothers weeping for their little babies and even for themselves; I can imagine the men feeling despondent, not knowing what to do, feeling incapacitated and thinking they were failures as they couldn't save their children or their wives. What a terrible state! Now they needed a change and they needed it so quickly and desperately else they would all be destroyed.

> *The desire for a change always comes when there is a challenge or trouble where you know that only God's intervention can get you out of such trouble*

Mordecai was so distressed and troubled that he went straight to the king's gate in his sackcloth to explain the matter at hand and its enormity to Queen Esther. On arriving there, he showed the king's eunuch the copy of the written decree for their destruction as evidence that something needed to be done, and urgently at that.

How could Esther have considered the fact that she was not authorized to go into the king except she was called upon. She didn't think for a second that the law spelt "all Jews" which included the queen herself, but thank God she was smart enough to change her mind to go in to the king especially after Mordecai spoke roughly to her.

Esther 4:11-15 reads:

> *All the king's servants, and the people of the king's provinces, do know, that whosoever, whether man or women, shall*

come unto the king into the inner court, who is not called, there is one law of his to put him to death, except such to whom the king shall hold out the golden sceptre, that he may live: but I have not been called to come in unto the king these thirty days.

And they told to Mordecai Esther's words.

Then Mordecai commanded to answer Esther, think not with thyself that thou shalt escape in the king's house, more than all the Jews.

For if thou altogether holdest thy peace at this time, then shall there enlargement and deliverance arise to the Jews from another place; but thou and thy father's house shall be destroyed: and who knoweth whether thou art come to the kingdom for such a time as this?

Then Esther bade them return Mordecai this answer

The intensity of the desire for a change had welled up so strongly within Esther that she was ready to lose her life just to save her people. She went into action by declaring a fast among the Jews for three days, after which she went into the inner court of the king. Of course, she found favour before the king, and the decree against the Jews was altered.

A desire always makes you swing into action

Another inspiring story to learn from is the woman with the issue of blood in Mathew 9:20-21:

And behold, a woman, which was diseased with an issue
of blood twelve years, came behind Him, and touched the
hem of His garment:

For she said within herself, If I may but touch His garment,
I shall be whole.

This is a good example of one who desired a change. For twelve long years, she had spent all her life savings on physicians because of a health condition of constant bleeding, and she desperately needed a miracle. I am thinking of how tired and ill-looking she would have been from losing so much blood. Today, this condition would have necessitated frequent hospital admissions to receive blood transfusions and intra-venous fluids to replace what she lost through bleeding. I can imagine her blood count being so low that she might have had a heart failure from anaemia. I can imagine her going into hypovolaemic shock. Though, the Bible did not clearly identify the many things she suffered from the physicians, medically speaking she would have had those conditions due to her constant blood loss. Isn't it baffling that despite all her savings being spent on the physicians (Luke 8:43), neither of them could heal her?

She had to look for Jesus, and her search ended when she met Him. What a day that was for her. The long-desired change of twelve years had finally come to an end.

When you come to Jesus, you have arrived, your
search halts because you have arrived home and a
new journey with Him begins

Something worth mentioning in verse 44 is the fact that she came behind Him and touched His garment. She had to go behind, perhaps because she was regarded as unclean and not fit to be among people, or because some would have thought she was cursed to have such a disease come upon her and wouldn't want to associate with her. So instead of walking up directly in front of Him, she decided to go behind quietly to touch His garment and leave unnoticed; knowing that Jesus was her final hope since the doctors were of no help. This woman is clearly someone who was desperate and desirous of a change. It was not just enough for her to hear that Jesus heals, but with her frail body, she took a step further to find the master and "touch Him". Note that touch here is an action word.

Again, a desire will always cause you to take bold steps

Another lesson to learn from this story is that the virtue in Jesus was intended for Jairus' daughter of whom Jesus was on His way to heal when this woman went for her own portion of miracle. She would not let anyone stop her from touching Jesus, and indeed her faith (which was moved by her actions) made her whole.

A real desire for a change will not consider limitations, hindrances, or oppositions

The story of Hannah will always be a reference for anyone who is going through a challenge and more than ever desires the power of God to bear on their situation to cause a change. Several women who needed the fruit of the womb have found solace in Hannah's story and applied the same principles, to get their miracle baby(ies).

Hannah's story points to God's faithfulness and kindness, reminding anyone who desires a change that God answers prayers and honors our desires for change.

In 1 Samuel 1:1-21, the bible mentions that she was married to Elkanah for years and could not bear a child, this made her sad. Her rival, Elkanah's other wife also made life unbearable for her. Perhaps she must have sought medical help, yet no physician could help; she knew that only God could bring about the change she desired in her life. It is also likely that because of the love her husband had for her compared to the other wife, Hannah would have relaxed or not see a dire need to have a child. However, the desire became strong when her rival provoked her severely and made her miserable. The Bible says that year after year when she went up to the House of the Lord, her rival provoked her till she wept and would not eat. This constant and persistent provocation and misery made Hannah desire an urgent change.

In verse 10-11

> *And she was in bitterness of soul, and prayed unto the Lord, and wept sore.*
>
> *And she vowed a vow, and said, O Lord of hosts, if thou wilt indeed look on the affliction of thine handmaid, and remember me, and not forget thine handmaid, but wilt give unto thine handmaid a man child, then I will give him unto the Lord all the days of his life, and there shall no razor come upon his head.*

Her strong and sincere desire led her to the place of prayer and to make a vow to God. She knew that God would always keep to His own bargain of the vow and that God takes vows seriously.

> *A strong desire for a change always drives you to pour out your soul to God, which God always rewards*

It is God's desire for you to be fulfilled and live a life of joy. He always draws our attention to His word; to ask of Him of whatever we desire so that our joy may be full (John 16:24). That is His earnest desire; that we be perfect and complete, lacking nothing.

Do you require a change in your life? Do you need a change in your situation? Are you going through a challenge and you have searched everywhere for help? Do you want God's power to produce results for you? Then you must have a desire that is strong enough to cause the change that you require.

> *No change really takes place without the desire for a change*

Perhaps you are in an awful state that desperately needs a change, but you are not really giving it a lot of attention. You need to realise that nothing will change if you don't make up your mind for a better life. Hannah could have probably made excuses for her predicament believing that one day God will give her a child and before she knew it years and years went by. Perhaps she could have consoled herself that her husband really did not mind if she had a child or not after all he said to her, "...*am I not better to you than ten sons?*" *(1 Samuel 1:8).*

The moment it dawned on her that those excuses will never change her state, she got a miracle which started with a strong desire. The same for Esther, she gave Mordecai an excuse that anyone not called into the inner courts of the king by the king himself would be killed. That was a justifiable excuse and reason to hold back. However, when Mordecai gave her a strict warning not to think that she will escape in the kings palace while the other Jews die, she had a rethink, and suddenly the desire for a change grew strong in her (Esther 4:13-14).

In Mark 10:46, the Bible gave account of the story of blind Bartimaeus who sat by the highway side begging and when he heard it was Jesus, he began to cry out saying Jesus the son of David have mercy on me.

In verse 51, Jesus asked him, *"what would thou that I should do unto thee"? The blind man said unto Him, Lord, that I might receive my sight.* Jesus knew even before the man asked what he wanted, but He wanted the desire to get healed to come from the blind man.

> *No one will ever persuade you for a change as much as yourself, it always must be from you*

Recognise the Need for a Change

A sincere desire for a change makes you uncomfortable with your present situation or state. You must first recognise the need for a change. Sometimes Christians go through several challenges or predicament without realising the need for an urgent change. Sometimes they allow the state to get so worse and deteriorate to a level that cannot be reversed. Do not be that way. Learn to be sensitive to things going on around you or your loved ones and be quick to seek for a change. Do not do in December what you should have done in January. Recognise the need for a change quickly and swing into action immediately.

Be Uncomfortable

When you recognise that you need to move to the next level of your life in which ever area you want, then the desire for that change begins to build and gather momentum in you, until all you think of is that next level. The strong desire makes you uncomfortable with your present status quo. When this happens, then you can be rest assured that you are on your way to change, to a higher level, to a more glorious state where you will have fulfillment in whatever you desire. It all starts by being uncomfortable with your present state. Do not wish for a change today and the next day, you are wondering if you should forget about it. It does not work that way. It will mean that you are unstable and the Bible states that an unstable man will not receive anything from the Lord (James 1:8).

Feed Your Desire

Let us look at David and how he fed his desire.

Psalm 63:1-2 says:

> *O God, thou art my God; early will I seek thee: my soul thirsteth for thee, my flesh longeth for thee in a dry and thirsty land, where no water is.*

> *To see thy power and thy glory, so as I have seen thee in the sanctuary.*

David fed his desire by seeking God in His word. Your desire for change will cause you to go in search of information which will help you grow your desire stronger and move you to the next level.

Mathew 5:6 says:

Blessed are they which do hunger and thirst after righteousness: for they shall be filled.

Do you want to know more about what God says about your situation and get your desired result? The more your hunger and thirst increases, the more your desire increases and the more results you see.

Your desire grows as much as how you feed it, a thin desire is starved and unfed

Protect Your Desire

John 10:10 (AMPC) says:

The thief cometh not, but for to steal, and to kill, and to destroy: I am come that they might have life, and that they might have it more abundantly.

You must consciously protect your desire, else you lose it, because there is a devil out there who would try to stop you from reaching your goals. Guard your desires in your heart and don't let fear and unbelief stop you.

Several years ago, I was desperate for a change just like Hannah did and I would not accept no for an answer. I knew that help would only come from God and I kept at it. I desired for a second child. After the first child, I tried to conceive for three years but nothing happened. I knew I had to get into the miraculous to get my miracle. I began to nurse that desire day after day, studying God's word and holding onto every promise God gave to women about having the fruit of the womb. Several nights, I would cry out loud to God in prayer and I never gave room for fear or doubt. I surrounded myself with God's word every day. I held on to my faith and the principles in God's word until I got my miracle. My desire was second to none and I sure got my miracle baby.

Do you have a desire for a change? How strong is your desire? Will you allow the enemy to take that desire away?

CHAPTER 2

ENEMIES OF CHANGE

We all want changes in our lives daily ranging from simple everyday routines such as changing our hairstyle, wardrobe, or diets, to changing complex things like ill health conditions, challenging situations at work, home, offices etc.

Everyone has one thing or the other that he/she wants to accomplish. I believe everyone desires to move to higher levels in every area of their lives; that is because we are unique and creators just like our heavenly Father. No one wants to be stagnant in life but desires to rise and make progress consistently.

To some people, it is easy to make these changes and to others, it may take a long time or may never happen. It is God's desire that His children attain greater heights, move from one level of success to the other, be it in their health, finances, relationships, marriages, or businesses etc. However, not everyone sees these dreams come into fruition because there is an enemy out there who tries to abort these dreams, if allowed.

Let us look at some enemies of change:

Fear

Some months ago, I read a book by a great woman of God: Joyce Meyer (Do it afraid) where she wrote about the right and the wrong kind of fear; the right kind of fear being the reverential fear and awe of God which doesn't mean being afraid of Him because He is going to hurt you. W.E Vine describes fear as a wholesome dread of displeasing God, and that which influences the disposition, and attitude of any one whose circumstances are guided by trust in God through the indwelling Spirit of God. Vine further stated that the reverential fear of God will inspire the constant carefulness in dealing with others.

1 Peter 2:17 says, *honour all men, love the Brotherhood, fear God, honour the King.* This is not our focus because it is the right kind of fear. It is just a pointer, so you can be clear on the kinds of fear. The focus in this book is the wrong kind of fear. The Greek word for fear is *"phobos"* which first had the meaning of "flight", that which is caused by being scared, that which may cause dread or terror. It is also defined as that which is caused by intimidation of adversaries.

Many people's lives are controlled by fear; all manner of fear ranging from fear of the future, fear of failing, fear of criticism, fear of mistakes, fear of the devil, fear of dark places and all kinds of fear. But you see, fear will never allow you to become the best of you. It will never allow you to make any progress in your life or see the light of your dreams. That is because fear is of the devil and it torments. I need you to understand this clearly that fear torments.

Let us look at 1 John 4:18.

> *There is no fear in love: but perfect love casted out fear because fear hath torment. He that feareth is not made perfect in love.*

The scripture explains it all. There is no fear in love because love is of God and God is love. Fear and love cannot co-exist because fear is of the devil. The Greek word for torment is *"kolasis"* and it means punishment, infliction, or anguish.

In Mathew 4:24,

> *And His fame went throughout all Syria: and they brought unto Him all sick people that were taken with divers diseases and torments, and those which were possessed with devils, and those which were lunatic, and those that had the palsy; and he healed them.*

Time and time again, God tells His children in His word "not to be afraid" because He knows the dangers and destructions that comes with fear. No wonder Paul said, *"For God hath not given us the Spirit of fear, but of power, and of love and of a sound mind"* (2 Timothy 1:7).

Fear is a spirit and that spirit is of the devil. Fear is a big hindrance and enemy of change. Rip fear out of your heart, do not take it easy with fear otherwise it will mess up with your dreams, aspirations, and life in general. Look at Job in the Bible. The Bible called him a perfect man, one who feared God (which is good) and eschewed evil but do you know also that Job was living in fear (the wrong kind of fear). How do I know you may ask?

What you fear eventually comes upon you

Let us look at Job 3:25-26:

> *For the thing which I greatly feared is come upon me, and that which I was afraid of is come unto me.*
>
> *I was not in safety, neither had I rest, neither was I quiet; yet trouble came.*

Read the above verses carefully and note the tenses. Job used the word "greatly feared", not something he feared lightly, but "greatly". Secondly, he said the word "feared" meaning past tense; a fear that has been there in the past. Then he goes on to say, "I was not in safety, neither had I rest".

Isn't it surprising how Job was described as perfect, but he did not know that he was protected of God? Even the devil knew that there was a hedge of protection about him. So how come Job did not know? Why did he have to say he was not in safety?

The knowledge of our union with God guarantees our safety

Let us read the account of Job in chapter one and see what the devil had to say about Job's safety, then you will truly understand that even the devil knew that Job was in safety.

Job 1:9-10 says:

> *Then Satan answered the LORD, and said, Doth Job fear God for nought?*

Hast not thou made a hedge about him, and about his house, and about all that he hath on every side? thou hast blessed the work of his hands, and his substance is increased in the land.

God richly blessed Job and blessed the works of his hands. The bible says,...*his substance also was seven thousand sheep, and three thousand camels and five hundred yoke of oxen and five hundred she asses and a very great household; so that this man was the greatest of all men of the East* (Job 1:3). Perhaps he thought, what if I lose all these blessings in one day? In Job 3:25, he said that which I greatly feared is come upon me; it is possible that he may have thought of losing this great wealth and wondered what would happen. He was living in fear.

Throughout my walk with God, He kept telling me, *"fear not, for I am with you"* (Isaiah 41:10). I recalled feeling pains in my lower abdomen some time ago. It was so intense that I was afraid of what it could be, but suddenly I heard the Spirit of God say loudly to me, *"fear not for I am with you"*. The pain persisted but over the few days as I kept declaring that word, the pain vanished completely. This is to let you know that perfect love casted out fear. Let go of fear and get a hold of God's love because fear will never allow you make any change or progress in your life.

The knowledge, consciousness and confession of God's word produces victory

Uncertainty

Uncertainty is another enemy of change that prevents people from living the upward and forward life that God has called them to live. At one time or the other, we may have been faced with uncertainties:

uncertain about what the future holds. Perhaps you just started a new job and feel overwhelmed at the challenges that stares at you and you are not sure if you are competent for the job. There are lot of things people can get uncertain about, but you must consciously put a stop to the negative emotions, which is an enemy of change and fix your gaze on Jesus. The very one who lives in you has assured you that He is greater than the uncertainty before you. When you put your trust in God you will not know when the heat of life comes (Jeremiah17: 8).

Paul says, *I therefore so run, not as uncertainly; so fight I, not as one that beateth the air* (1 Corinthians 9: 26). *He who did not spare His own son but gave Him up for us, how will He not also with Him graciously give us all things* (Romans 8:32). God has covered you in His loving arms and endless provisions and desires that you trust Him because you will always hear a word saying- this is the way, walk ye in it.

God says in Isaiah 49:15, *"Would you give birth to a child and forget to feed or care for your own child? No, you won't, but even if you do, God says He will not forget you"*. He has good plans towards you, plans for welfare and not for evil, to give you a future and hope (Jeremiah 29:11), so put your trust in God and stop being uncertain.

Unforgiveness

Sometimes, we find it difficult to forgive ourselves when we make mistakes. It is easy for us to forgive others, but we become hard on ourselves when we make an error. We tend to be our hardest critics, beating up ourselves even when others have forgiven us. God wants you to forgive yourself as much as you forgive others and learn from your mistakes so that you can move forward in life and make progress.

Not forgiving yourself makes you your own enemy

Philippians 3:13 says:

> *Brethren, I count not myself to have apprehended: but this*
> *one thing I do, forgetting those things which are behind,*
> *and reaching forth unto those things which are before.*

Paul could have found reasons to be hard on himself considering how he persecuted Christians.

Let us look at Philippians 3:13 from the Passion translation:

> *I do not depend on my own strength to accomplish this;*
> *however, I do have one compelling focus: I forget all of the*
> *past as I fasten my heart to the future instead.*

Holding on to the past was certainly going to hinder Paul's ministry to the gentiles, therefore he was compelled not to allow the habits in his past stop his ministry or prevent him from answering the call of God upon his life. I can imagine that there was guilt in his heart and the accuser of the brethren (Satan) constantly reminding him of all he did and how he is not fit to preach the gospel; perhaps, it was such a battle *but he made a compelling focus* to leave the past behind and fasten His heart to the future. You've got to make up your mind to have a compelling focus to let go of the past. Your focus must be so strong and compelling to the extent that it overwhelms and overshadows your past, then you can really say that you are ready for a change. You cannot hold onto the past and see the new thing that God is ready to do for you and you can't have change while living in your past failures and mistakes.

Just maybe you have been living wrongly, getting into all kinds of troubles, making life difficult both for yourself and for the world around you. Maybe you have rejected Jesus as the Lord of your life and now your life is in a mess; what you need now is a new way of life which only Jesus can give. You will have to let go of your pains and come to Him so He can wash you clean with His blood and His word; this is the greatest change anyone can make- the change from the Kingdom of darkness to the kingdom of His son.

The future will remain bleak if the past is within reach

Giving Up

When you give up in life because of a certain challenge you are faced with, you will never reach the full potentials of what God has in store for you. There are times when things are not working out the way you expect, when things just do not seem right despite your efforts. At such times, you may be tempted to give up on that dream, vision, or goal which you had set out your heart towards. That is exactly what the devil wants you to do; resist Him and he will flee from you. *Do you not know that in a race, all the runners run, but only one receives the price so run that you may obtain it?* (1 Corinthians 9:24). Don't give up!

Also look at James 1:12, it says:

> *Blessed is the man that endureth temptation: for when he is tried, he shall receive the crown of life, which the Lord hath promised to them that love Him.*

You can trust that the Holy Spirit in you will guide you all the way until you achieve that dream. He said to Jacob, I will not leave you until I have done all I have said concerning you (Genesis 28:15). It even makes it more beautiful for those of us who are born again Christians who have the Holy Ghost in us forever. Do not ever give up in the face of daunting situations and do not give in either, for this will prevent you from making your desired change, reaching your goals and aspirations in life.

Let us look at an interesting verse in Isaiah:

Isaiah 41:10 (AMPC)

> *Fear not [there is nothing to fear], for I am with you; do not look around you in terror and be dismayed, for I am your God. I will strengthen and harden you to difficulties, yes, I will help you; yes, I will hold you up and retain you with My [victorious] right hand of rightness and justice.*

Your present state, dilemma is nothing. God calls it nothing and so must you. He gives you the assurance and reasons not to fear because He is with you, how comforting that is. This is one scripture that has changed the course of my life. God is saying to you, do not look around in terror, dismayed and pacing the floor wondering who to call or what to do but rather be bold. Why does He want you to be bold? because the Almighty God, the Monarch of the universe, the one who created all things is with you, and if He says He is with you, then you have it made. I love the rendering in the Amplified version which says "I will Harden you to difficulties" meaning despite the challenges that you are in at the moment, He will toughen you so hard that you are unperturbed or unshakeable.

Let us look at the same scripture from the good news Bible. It reads, *do not be afraid, I am with you. I am your God- let nothing terrify you. I will make you strong and help you; I will protect you and save you.*

If we will trust Him for who He is, He will help us with what we are not

When you go through that challenge, He will do four things for you from the above scripture:

1. Strengthen you
2. Help you
3. Protect you (from the harm of the challenge)
4. Save (deliver) you

It couldn't get easier and better than this, to know that you have a God who watches out for you to protect you from troubles, and that He is there with you all the way. It's so comforting and amazing!

Isaiah 41:13 *says "I am the Lord your God, I strengthen you and do not be afraid, I will help you"*

The Living Bible *says, "I am holding you by your right hand- I the Lord your God- and I say to you (reinforcing it) do not be afraid; I am here to help you"*

According to the Living Bible translation, "I am holding you" is not futuristic, not a promise but a present hour reality. You don't need to be disturbed about how you are going to come out of that ordeal because He is right there to help you according to His word. You can trust His word with your life. He says to you, do not be afraid, I am here, not far away, not in "heaven" but right here. Is He here to judge you? No, but to help you.

Romans 8:28 says, *...and we know that all things work together for good to them that love God, to them who are the called according to His purpose.* This should comfort you even further on the need to hold on, to keep going on, to stay strong and not to give up.

> *All the pains you go through were fashioned to make you stronger if only you believe*

Procrastination

When we avoid making the necessary changes in our lives and circumstances either by procrastinating or giving up, we suffer the consequences. We must consciously give ourselves to discipline and diligence to attain the heights of success and victory.

Hebrews 12:11 (AMPC) says:

> *For the time being no discipline brings joy, but seems grievous and painful; but afterwards it yields a peaceable fruit of righteousness to those who have been trained by it [a harvest of fruit which consists in righteousness—in conformity to God's will in purpose, thought, and action, resulting in right living and right standing with God].*

A lazy hand makes for poverty, but diligent hands bring wealth (Proverbs 10:4). When you procrastinate, you are giving room for poverty. The scripture we just read says it "makes", that means "allows for" poverty. Do not make room for poverty. A dear man of God once said, "don't do in December what you should have done in January". As the scripture rightly said, only the lazy hands make for poverty. Those who make excuses will never make it in life. They will never see change let alone live the life that they desired to live. In anything you set out to do, ensure that your goals are realistic, give yourself to discipline and determination, and see to it that those dreams, projects, and desires come to reality. That is the only way you can make progress in life.

Psalm 90:12 says, *teach us to number our days that we might apply our hearts to wisdom.*

Wealth is produced when we desire and embrace wisdom

God wants us to apply our hearts to wisdom in doing what we said we would do. When you procrastinate, you reduce your effectiveness in doing that which you are meant to do. Solomon gave several words of wisdom about dangers of procrastination that we can learn from. *Every hard work brings profits but mere talk leads to poverty* (Proverbs 14:23).

From the above scripture, we can see the outcome of procrastination. It always leads to poverty and that is not God's desire and plan for His children.

Wrong Associations

The people we relate with have an influence over our thoughts, decision making, attitudes and way of life. Often there are people who have a negative effect on your morality and decision making. Such people will prevent you from making desired changes in your life. Paul admonishes us not to be misled, because bad company corrupts good manners (1 Corinthians 15:33).

The company you surround yourself with has a direct impact on your life and will change the direction of your journey. Every friendship you keep has the potential to determine or influence your destiny. The company you keep determines what accompanies you. If you walk with the wise, you will certainly become wise (Proverbs 22:24-25). You cannot hang out with negative people and expect to live a positive life. It is time to leave that circle of friends because negativity and positivity can never coexist. Get the wrong people out of your life!

A wrong association will always remain a hindrance to success

Negative Thoughts

The first place where change takes place is in the mind. You are exactly what you think. The Bible says: *For as a man think it in his heart so is he...* (Proverbs 23:7). If you think success, then you will certainly succeed. Jesus said: *A good man out of the good treasures in His heart bringeth forth that which is good.* (Luke 6: 45).

In Romans 12:2, the Bible says:

> *And be not conformed to this world but be transformed by the renewing of your mind, that you may prove what is that good, and acceptable and perfect will of God.*

How important this is. If only we would put this simple truth to work, we will experience the miraculous in our lives through the power of our minds. Paul lets us know that God gave us our minds for our transformation, to change the way we think, and be transported to another level. The Greek word is *"metamorphoo"* which means to transform, to be transfigured, to change into another form, to metamorphose.

Now God has told us how to cause this transformation. He said by the renewing of our minds. He never asked you to renew any material thing (as good as they are) but rather he asked you to renew your mind because if you do, those things you desire will follow. He designed our minds for transformation. The material to use in renewing your mind is God's word, not the news, not the suggestions from friends, not other people's experiences but with the word of God. Why? Because the more you look at the word of God, you are being ***transformed*** *into the same image from glory to glory even asked by the Spirit of the Lord* (2 Corinthians 3:18).

For instance, if someone who is sick looks at this scripture, *"He was wounded for our transgressions, He was bruised for our iniquities, the chastisement of our peace upon Him and by His wounds were healed"*(Isaiah 53:5), he will be transformed completely and will receive his healing. This is how to transform and renew your mind. When you do this, you can be sure that change is inevitable.

Doubt

Doubt is another enemy of change that can bring fear and distrust. When you doubt God's word for you, you give room for fear to creep into your life and that replaces the faith you had. As long as you walk in doubt, you will not see the manifestations of the power of God in your life, *for without faith it is impossible to please Him: for He that cometh to God must believe that He is, and that He is a rewarder of them that diligently seek Him* (Hebrews 11:6).

Look at Mathew 14:28-31,

> *And Peter answered Him and said, Lord, if it be, thou bid me come unto thee on the water.*
>
> *And he said, Come. And when Peter was come down out of the ship, he walked on the water, to go to Jesus.*
>
> *But when he saw the wind boisterous, he was afraid; and beginning to sink, he cried, saying, Lord, save me.*
>
> *And immediately Jesus stretched forth His hand, and caught him, and said unto him, O thou of little faith, wherefore didst thou doubt?*

If peter fixed his gaze on Jesus, he would have continued walking on the water but the moment he took his eyes off the master to the wind, he became afraid. Do not lose focus of your dreams and aspirations, no matter how dark the night may seem, joy will surely come in the morning. Most importantly, do not lose your focus on Jesus. Maintain your gaze on Him for He is *the author and perfecter of your faith* (Hebrews 12:2). He knows exactly how to bring you out of that trouble, and you can always trust Him.

Doubt always give room to fear

Mark 11:23 reads,

> *For verily I say unto you, that whosoever shall say to this*
> *mountain, be thou removed and be thou cast into the sea*
> *and shall not DOUBT in his heart, but shall believe that*
> *those thing which he saith, shall come to pass, he shall have*
> *WHATSOEVER he saith.*

Doubt is a great enemy of change. Never entertain or negotiate with doubt. Once you locate what God says in the word about your situation, take a leap of faith and hold strongly unto what the word says, and you will have what you say.

CHAPTER 3

FRIENDS OF CHANGE

I n this chapter, I will be discussing some of the fruits of the Spirit, which are friends of change. Change is possible when we have the right mindset towards it and apply the principles of God's word. You must understand that God's desire for you, is to live a successful and prosperous life. That is the reason why He came. God is never satisfied until you are satisfied because your joy is His joy. Think about how much a mother loves her child and will do anything to make sure that her child is happy. It is the same thing and much more with our Heavenly Father. You need to believe it and know that He loves you so much that He made you one with Himself. Therefore, you should take advantage of His grace and put the word of God to work.

Faith

Faith is one of the friends of change. When you act your faith, nothing is impossible onto you. Faith never fails. If you wanted something and you did not get it, then you did not put your faith to work, because faith always works.

Think about it, the Bible says these three shall abide.

1 Corinthians 13:13 reads:

> *And now these three remain: Faith, hope, and love. But the greatest of this is love.*

That means, forever these three, will always remain even when everything else fails. Love is the greatest which is very beautiful but the only one which God said we must have to please Him, is faith.

Faith abides where love and hope reside

Hebrews 11:6 says:

> *But without faith it is impossible to please Him: for he that cometh to God must believe that he is, and that he is a rewarder of them that diligently seek Him.*

Faith never fails. If you have faith, happy are you because you can change anything and that is why you are reading this book. It is not about the size of your faith. Someone may say: "I have very little faith; I doubt if it will work". The Bible says, *if you have faith as small as the mustard seed, you shall say to this mountain, move from here to there and it will move. Nothing shall be impossible unto you* (Matthew 17:20).

The more you exercise your faith by putting it to work, the more your faith grows. Don't be the one to delay the change you desire to move you to higher realms in your life. All you need is available to you. The word is near you; it is in your mouth and in your heart. You can change just about anything, no matter how small your faith is.

Let us take it deeper and further. If you are not satisfied with the little faith that you have (even though Jesus says nothing shall be impossible unto you), you can grow your faith. The Bible talks of little faith, weak faith, great faith, and strong faith.

Luke 7:9 reads:

> *When Jesus had these things, he marvelled at him and turn*
> *him about and say it onto the people that followed Him, I*
> *say to you, I have not found so great faith, no, not in Israel.*

Jesus acknowledged that there is such a thing as great faith. Amazing!

Paul talks about weak faith and strong faith in Romans 4:19:

> *And being not weak in faith, he considered not his own*
> *body now dead, but was strong in faith, giving glory*
> *to God.*

How do you get your faith to be strong and great? It is by hearing more of God's word. *For faith cometh by hearing and hearing by the word of God* (Romans10:17). Whether it is little or great, it will change your circumstances, and nothing shall be impossible unto you.

Abraham displayed strong faith in God even though he didn't have a son.

The Bible says in Romans 4: 18-22:

> *Who against hope believed in hope, that he might become*
> *the father of many nations, according to that which was*
> *spoken, so shall thy seed be.*

> *And being not weak in faith, he considered not his own body now dead, when he was about an hundred years old, neither yet the deadness of Sarah's womb:*

> *He staggered not at the promise of God through unbelief; but was strong in faith, giving glory to God.*

> *And being fully persuaded that, what he had promised, he was able also to perform. And therefore, it was imputed to him for righteousness.*

Are you fully persuaded of His love and faithfulness? You must have faith in God because faith never fails.

Full persuasion produces undeniable results

Hebrews 11:32-35 says:

> *And what shall I more say? for the time would fail me to tell of Gedeon, and of Barak, and of Samson, and of Jephthae; of David also, and Samuel, and of the prophets:*

> *Who through faith subdued kingdoms, wrought righteousness, obtained promises, stopped the mouths of lions,*

> *Quenched the violence of fire, escaped the edge of the sword, out of weakness were made strong, waxed valiant in fight, turned to flight the armies of the aliens.*

Women received their dead raised to life again: and others were tortured, not accepting deliverance; that they might obtain a better resurrection:

You can achieve anything by faith. You change and become anything by faith. Apply the faith principle today and see your life soar high as the eagles.

Humility

Humility is a virtue that is priceless and precious. Humility is accepting God's word even when your circumstances looks different from the word of God. Pride is when you refuse to receive His word as He says. God always resist the proud and gives grace to the humble.

Take for instance, if you are sick in your body and desperate about your situation, and God's word comes to you (as it is now), saying to you, that none in Zion shall say they are sick (Isaiah 33:24), you should immediately receive that word and see yourself well even though you still feel the symptoms. If you accept that word, before long every symptom will disappear; that's because God's word never fails, and He cannot lie (Romans 3:4 and Numbers 23:19).

2 chronicles 7:14 says:

If my people who are called by my name will humble themselves and pray and seek my face and turn from their wicked ways, then I will hear from heaven and I will forgive their sin and will heal their land.

If you will humble yourself and turn to Him in prayer with a honest and sincere heart, willing to unlearn all that is inconsistent with His word and learn His word and His ways, then change is possible for you even now.

Change is inevitable in humility

The Bible speaks highly of Moses who had this priceless virtue.

Numbers 12:3 reads:

> *Now Moses was a very humble man, more humble than anyone else on the face of the earth.*

That is because Moses acknowledged and obeyed God in all His ways. He saw himself subservient to God's greater authority and wisdom. No wonder he was found worthy and used of God to bring the Israelites out of Egypt.

Can we exhaust this virtue enough? Understand that there is greatness in humility. Think of Jesus, whose humility is unfathomable.

Recall in John 1: 1-4, Jesus had been with God since the beginning of time. Let us look at this together:

> *In the beginning was the Word, and the Word was with God, and the Word was God.*

> *The same was in the beginning with God.*

> *All things were made by Him; and without Him was not anything made that was made.*

> *In Him was life; and the life was the light of men.*

Think about this; when Jesus walked on the streets of the earth, He looked just like everyone else, yet He was God Himself. He was the God that called out to Moses in the burning bush and told Moses to take off His shoes, for the place where he stood was holy (Exodus 3:5).

He was Himself God, yet He chose to come to this earth and agreed to be treated like a common man.

Read this account in Philippians 2:6-8 (AMPC)

> *Who, although being essentially one with God and in the form of God [possessing the fullness of the attributes which make God God], did not think this equality with God was a thing to be eagerly grasped or retained,*

> *But stripped Himself [of all privileges and rightful dignity], so as to assume the guise of a servant (slave), in that He became like men and was born a human being.*

> *And after He had appeared in human form, He abased and humbled Himself [still further] and carried His obedience to the extreme of death, even the death of the cross!*

Humility is walking with God and accepting His word. Humility will not only enable you cause changes in your life, but will take you far in life, far into success, far unto greater Heights.

Verse 9-11 is so beautiful and shows us the reward of humility.

> *Therefore [because He stooped so low] God has highly exalted Him and has freely bestowed on Him the name that is above every name,*

That in (at) the name of Jesus every knee should (must) bow, in heaven and on earth and under the earth,

And every tongue [frankly and openly] confess and acknowledge that Jesus Christ is Lord, to the glory of God the Father.

The reward of humility is greatness and authority

Honesty

The Greek word for honesty is "*kalos*" which means good, admirable, fair, right, honourable, of such conduct as deserves esteem. Honesty is marked as being free from deceit. It is described as sincere. Honesty is an important virtue in making changes in your life. To be honest means, to be sincere with yourself. You need this as a friend of change. You must be true to yourself and come to God just the way you are, not trying to act as though you have it all covered when you know you do not. It means you must be sincere enough to ask for His help and accept that help from Him, for truly without Him, you can do nothing (John 15:51).

Let us look at some scriptures.

Proverbs 11:3 says:

The integrity of the upright guides them, but the unfaithful are destroyed by their duplicity.

Philippians 4:8-9 (AMPC):

For the rest, brethren, whatever is true, whatever is worthy of reverence and is honourable and seemly, whatever is just, whatever is pure, whatever is lovely and lovable, whatever is kind and winsome and gracious, if there is any virtue and excellence, if there is anything worthy of praise, think on and weigh and take account of these things [fix your minds on them].

Practice what you have learned and received and heard and seen in me, and model your way of living on it, and the God of peace (of untroubled, undisturbed well-being) will be with you.

Have a sincere heart to communicate to God exactly what you are going through and be ready to receive His help in other to make the necessary changes in your life.

A pure heart is a heart that pleases God

Focus

The Miriam Webster dictionary defines focus as a centre of activity, attraction, a point of concentration; a directed attention, a state or condition permitting clear perception or understanding.

In making changes in your life and achieving your set goals, you will need to be very focused in the direction you are going, and in the change that you want to make.

There will be many things to distract you; news of terror, wrong advices from friends and the list goes on and on. You must make up your mind to stay determined and focused. If you are not focused, then you are unstable, and you will not be able to receive anything from God nor make the changes you so desire (James 1: 8).

The Bible says in Hebrews 12:1-2 (AMPC):

> *Therefore then, since we are surrounded by so great a cloud of witnesses [who have borne testimony to the Truth], let us strip off and throw aside every encumbrance (unnecessary weight) and that sin which so readily (deftly and cleverly) clings to and entangles us, and let us run with patient endurance and steady and active persistence the appointed course of the race that is set before us,*

> *Looking away [from all that will distract] to Jesus, who is the Leader and the Source of our faith [giving the first incentive for our belief] and is also its Finisher [bringing it to maturity and perfection]. He, for the joy [of obtaining the prize] that was set before Him, endured the cross, despising and ignoring the shame, and is now seated at the right hand of the throne of God.*

The scripture makes it very clear on how to stay focused; you must strip yourself of every unnecessary weight. It is unnecessary because they are not needed in your journey to the new level.

Your past must be stripped off because it is a weight that is not needed. The pains, disappointment and frustrations of the past must be stripped off you completely. Failure to put away the distractions, will cause an entangling with your focus and render your plans useless.

There is a race to run and it is right before you. You must run valiantly with focus, so you can reach the finished line. That finished line is the change you desire, so go for it.

Distraction is a great enemy of change

Paul said in 1 Corinthians 9:26-27:

> *I therefore so run, not as uncertainly; so, fight I, not as one that beateth the air:*

> *But I keep under my body and bring it into subjection: lest that by any means, when I have preached to others, I myself should be a castaway.*

Paul was determined and focused in fulfilling the ministry God gave to him. He trained Timothy and everyone who followed him to do the same. He did not only preach about staying focused in Christ, he lived it out as well. Did he succeed in his ministry? Emphatically yes. And so, will you if you make focus your friend.

Focus never looks around and does not consider the present circumstances neither is it swaddled by distractions

Patience

Patience is a worthy virtue in the Christian walk and a fruit of the Spirit which must be imbibed by all. It is vital in trusting God when things do not go as smoothly as you want.

Habakkuk 2:2-3 says:

And the LORD answered me, and said, Write the vision, and make it plain upon tables, that he may run that readeth it.

For the vision is yet for an appointed time, but at the end it shall speak, and not lie: though it tarry, wait for it; because it will surely come, it will not tarry.

When you desire a change in your life, the Bible admonishes that you must write your vision (the change you want to see), so it can always be before you as a constant reminder and all who see it will run along with it. It also says that you should wait for it; to wait for the change. Even though it tarries, it doesn't mean it has been denied, it just means that you should wait a little longer.

Patience always waits for the result

Patience is never in a rush. Patience does not make haste, *for they that believe shall not make haste* (Isaiah 28:16).

Let us see what happened to someone in the Bible who was not patient and did not give room for patience to complete a perfect walk in his life.

1 Samuel 13:8-14:

And he tarried seven days, according to the set time that Samuel had appointed: but Samuel came not to Gilgal; and the people were scattered from him.

And Saul said, Bring hither a burnt offering to me, and peace offerings. And he offered the burnt offering.

And it came to pass, that as soon as he had made an end of offering the burnt offering, behold, Samuel came; and Saul went out to meet him, that he might salute him.

And Samuel said, what hast thou done? And Saul said, Because I saw that the people were scattered from me, and that thou camest not within the days appointed, and that the Philistines gathered themselves together at Michmash;

Therefore said I, The Philistines will come down now upon me to Gilgal, and I have not made supplication unto the LORD: I forced myself therefore and offered a burnt offering.

The end of patience is perfection and completeness

Verse 13-14 further reads,

And Samuel said to Saul, thou hast done foolishly: thou hast not kept the commandment of the LORD thy God, which he commanded thee: for now would the LORD have established thy kingdom upon Israel for ever.

But now thy kingdom shall not continue: the LORD hath sought Him a man after His own heart, and the LORD hath commanded him to be captain over His people, because thou hast not kept that which the LORD commanded thee.

Saul was the king over Israel at a time and their enemy, the philistines had gathered to fight Israel. The Israelites became distressed for they were in danger and hid in caves, in thickets, holes and pits. Samuel the prophet told King Saul to wait for him in Gilgal so that he might offer a burnt offering to God upon his arrival. However, Saul was not patient enough to wait for Saul's arrival. He offered the burnt offering himself and the consequence of that made him lose his kingdom. How painful to know that many have lost their miracles because they gave up just at the point when the miracle was so close. They would not let patience have its way in their situations to the end.

Patience craves for time to see the outcome

Do not be that way. There is too much to lose when you are in haste. Patience will take you to your destination if you allow her. Be patient and wait for the timing because there is always a timing in change.

The destination of patience is satisfaction

CHAPTER 4

THE DEMANDS OF CHANGE

To make a change, there are qualities and principles that are demanded for a successful outcome. Let us explore some of the demands of change.

The Demand of Courage

Change is natural and sometimes may not be fun as we move from one phase of our lives to the other. It means letting go of the past and accepting the new level that you want to see. You must allow the comfortable to be replaced by new urgencies, and that will take place with courage.

The Greek word for courage is *"tharos"* which means to be of good cheer, to be confident, to be bold. Therefore, it is required of you to conquer all fears and live a life of courage and determination in life.

Have you ever been in a situation where you outlined several dreams you wanted actualised, you were excited about them, told everyone about your dreams and looked forward to it every day, then it was time to take actions but you realised that the dreams looked more difficult than you envisioned;

you decided to wait a few days to get more information, but you didn't; a few days turned into a few weeks, few weeks turned into months and gradually the passion for that dream waned and eventually died.

The missing link between the vision and its reality was courage. Whenever courage is missing, fear is in abundant supply. We have already discussed how to eradicate fear out of your life by meditating more on God's word and putting His words to work through faith.

Courage is a propeller

Let us looks at a few scriptures together.

Joshua 1:6-7:

> *Be strong and of a good courage: for unto this people shalt thou divide for an inheritance the land, which I swore unto their fathers to give them.*

> *Only be thou strong and very courageous, that thou mayest observe to do according to all the law, which Moses my servant commanded thee: turn not from it to the right hand or to the left, that thou mayest prosper withersoever thou goest.*

Joshua 1:9-11 further reads: *Have not I commanded you? Be strong, vigorous, and very courageous. Be not afraid, neither be dismayed, for the Lord your God is with you wherever you go.*

Here, God commands Joshua to be strong and courageous after the death of Moses. He knew Joshua will not be able to lead a stiff-necked people like the children of Israel (Exodus 32:9). These were people who would murmur and complain to Moses at the slightest opportunity, let alone Joshua who was a new leader. God had to resound it into Joshua's ears again and again on the need to be courageous, and not only courageous but *very* courageous. How important courage is in the actualization of our dreams and visions. It almost seems that a desired change will not take place without courage.

In verse 7 above,

God says something striking: "that you may observe to do". Courage makes you "do". You cannot have courage and lag; they don't go together. Once you have courage, you will automatically "do" by swinging into action. I believe you would have already eradicated fear from the points you learned in chapter 2, and now it's time to put on the garment of courage. Get up and act because courage has come.

Courage is that force that pushes you to action

The Demand of Discipline

Hebrews 12:10-11 (NIV) says:

They disciplined us for a little while as they thought best; but God disciplines us for our good, in order that we may share in His holiness.

No discipline seems pleasant at the time, but painful. Later on, however, it produces a harvest of righteousness and peace for those who have been trained by it.

No discipline is pleasant at the time just like the Bible states but the harvest or reward of it is priceless. Every discipline is an act of love. Think about it for a moment, you discipline your children when they do wrong or misbehave, because you want the best for them. You want them to be useful both to themselves and the society. You want them to have the right character and personality and become responsible, so when you correct them for wrongdoing, it is because you love them and want the best for them.

Just as you do to your children, it is also expected of you to do the same to yourself. You need to give yourself to training, instructions and corrections. No change can be possible without discipline. It is one of the perquisites for change. Change demands it, change deserves it and change is calling out for it.

A student who is preparing for exams will have to subject himself to discipline and dedicate more time to study, otherwise failure is inevitable for such a student. In the same way, one who desires change must subject himself to discipline before the desired results can be seen.

Hebrews 12:5-8 says:

> *And have you completely forgotten this word of encouragement that addresses you as a father addresses His son? It says, "My son, do not make light of the Lord's discipline, and do not lose heart when he rebukes you,*
>
> *because the Lord disciplines the one he loves, and he chastens everyone he accepts as His son.⁷ Endure hardship as discipline; God is treating you as His children. For what children are not disciplined by their father?⁸ If you are not*

disciplined—and everyone undergoes discipline—then you
are not legitimate, not true sons and daughters at all.

The scripture above instructs you never to make light of God's discipline. In your journey and walk with the lord, you will always be directed and reproved when you go wrong, that's because God has given us the Holy Spirit for our benefit to guide us, counsel us, and direct us. He seeks to help you turn out just the way God wants you to, but you must be willing to allow Him direct you and give yourself to His discipline. Come to think of it, anyone who is not disciplined, is not legitimate- not a true son or daughter.

Jesus said in John 12:26 (AMPC):

But the Comforter (Counsellor, Helper, Intercessor, Advocate, Strengthener, Standby), the Holy Spirit, Whom the Father will send in My name [in My place, to represent Me and act on My behalf], He will teach you all things. And He will cause you to recall (will remind you of, bring to your remembrance) everything I have told you.

Isaiah 30:21 says:

And thine ears shall hear a word behind thee, saying, this is the way, walk ye in it, when ye turn to the right hand, and when ye turn to the left.

You receive discipline from God through His word and through the counsel of the Holy Spirit which He gives to you from within. When you open your heart to receive it, your harvest will be inevitable. Nothing, and no demon can stop you from the higher life that God has called you in to. Give yourself to discipline because in so doing, you will be fully ready and prepared for your desired change.

The result of discipline is reigning

The Demand of Consistency

The Merriam Webster dictionary defines consistency as a steady continuity, showing steady conformity to character, believe or custom.

For any change to take place, in your life your attitude on your desired change must conform; there must be sync. Change demands that you show continuous, steady progress in conformity to what you desire. You must never be found wavering or doubting because it reduces the strength of consistency and eventually paralyses it.

If you set out to go to the gymnastics every evening to exercise so you could lose some weight (which is a desired change), then you must keep at it regularly just like you pledged in your heart until you lose that weight. This applies to anything and everything you want to change; be it in your health, finances, job, family etc.

Doubt weakens the strength of consistency

The Bible says in James 1:7,

> *Every good gift and every perfect gift is from above, and cometh down from the Father of lights, with whom is no variableness, neither shadow of turning.*

God does not waver and His gift towards us is not subject to change and has no variation. He is ever consistent in His will, His word, and

His way. He desires that we become just as perfect as He is (Matthew 5:48). So, regularity and consistency are very possible because this is the life you have been called to live and change demands it.

Hebrews 6:17-18 (AMPC) says:

Accordingly, God also, in His desire to show more convincingly and beyond doubt to those who were to inherit the promise the unchangeableness of His purpose and plan, intervened (mediated) with an oath.

This was so that, by two unchangeable things [His promise and His oath] in which it is impossible for God ever to prove false or deceive us, we who have fled [to Him] for refuge might have mighty indwelling strength and strong encouragement to grasp and hold fast the hope appointed for us and set before [us].

This verse describes the immutability of God's counsel meaning that His purpose is **not capable of being changed,** such that He confirmed it with an oath.

In other words, His promise is fixed, hard-and-fast, unalterable, incommutable. That is exactly how your mindset and character should be in making a change; the only thing you see, hear and say is "I can do".

No matter how dark the sky is, let the wind blow, let the sun cease to shine but you will remain immutable and unalterable concerning your change. Glory to God!

An immutable desire is result not denied

The Demand of Perseverance

Perseverance means continued effort to do something or achieve something despite the difficulties, failure, or opposition. The one who perseveres knows that the test and trials will produce steadfastness. No matter how tough the road may seem, do not give up. Remain steadfast and determined until your dreams come alive. God did not promise us that we will not go through difficulties, but He promised that He will be with us when we go through those moments.

Let us look at more scriptures,

Isaiah 41:10 says:

> *Fear thou not; for I am with thee: be not dismayed; for I am thy God: I will strengthen thee; yea, I will help thee; yea, I will uphold thee with the right hand of my righteousness.*

Isaiah 43:2 reads:

> *When thou passest through the waters, I will be with thee; and through the rivers, they shall not overflow thee: when thou walkest through the fire, thou shalt not be burned; neither shall the flame kindle upon thee.*

Refuse to look back when you encounter oppositions, even when there is no support from your loved ones and friends. Remain steadfast and persevere to the end. Be undaunted and unwavering, so that you can receive the end of your faith.

In Isaiah 43:5, God says, *"fear not for I am with you; I will bring thy seed from the East and gather them from the West...."*

When God tells you "fear not", that is because He is with you. He said, He will never leave us nor forsake us. That should give you confidence and assurance that no matter what you are going through, you are not alone. He is with you and in you all the way. He is the monarch of the universe. Who can hold a charge against God's elect? (Romans 8:33).

You are untouchable and nothing is powerful enough so defeat you. He won it all and gave you the victory. He disarmed principalities and powers, made a public spectacle of them, triumphing over them all for you, so hold your head high up for the trials did not come to drown you; they came to pass.

2 Corinthians 4:17-18says:

> *For our light affliction, which is but for a moment, worketh for us a far more exceeding and eternal weight of glory.*
>
> *While we look not at the things which are seen, but at the things which are not seen: for the things which are seen are temporal; but the things which are not seen are eternal.*

Notice something striking here. The Bible calls the affliction you are going through "light" and short-lived troubles.

The Amplified version calls it the light distress of the passing hour. They came to pass and never to be compared to the glory that should follow. Do not give up and do not give in, the one in you and with you is the greatest; He is right by your side for your advantage.

Who has prevented Him that He should repair, who is able to stand before Him? Whatever is under the whole heaven belongs to Him (Job 41:10-11). You are a joint heir with Christ so refuse to give in or give up but rather persevere.

Perseverance carries with it a heavy weight of glory

The Demand of Time

Habakkuk 2:3 reads:

> *For the vision is yet for an appointed time, but at the end it shall speak, and not lie though it tarry, wait for it; because it will surely come, it will not tarry.*

This verse is so comforting and reminds us of the need to wait. We learnt extensively on the importance of patience as an important ingredient in making change.

Patience flies on the wings of time

Let us dissect this verse a little further.

For every vision (dream, project, plan), there is an appointed time, an appointed season. There is timing with and in change which you must be acquainted with. Change demands that you allow time to perfect your dreams. An example is when you sow a mango seed, do you go back to the farm the next day to harvest it? Certainly not, for the principle of seed sowing is that the seed will first die, before it germinates and then bring forth much fruits (John 12: 24)

You will destroy the potentials for the seed to produce fruits when you do not give the seed time. The change will be immature if you deny it of it's time to go through the seasons and times before it produces fruits.

Another good example is a pregnant woman who carries a baby and is expected to give birth; the appointed time for a pregnancy is nine months. If that woman gives birth any time before nine months, that baby will be immature with significant health risk, and increased chances of death. In the same vein, change must be allowed to mature to its full potentials to bring forth life and the desired results.

Ecclesiastes 3:11 says:

> *He hath made everything beautiful in His time: also, he hath set the world in their heart, so that no man can find out the work that God maketh from the beginning to the end.*

The scripture says that God makes everything beautiful in His time. Let us take for instance, you desire a change in your relationship, you desire to move from just dating into getting married to the person you love; don't be in such a hurry to make that decision because others are getting married as though you are in a competition. Give yourself the time necessary to understand your spouse to be; at the right time, your desire will come to pass. There is no reason to hurry and make hasty decisions. Avoiding going through the process will mean making mistakes on the long run. Allow yourself to go through the seasons and times; at the end of it, your desire will be perfect, mature, and complete.

Someone may ask, how will I know the time? The answer to your question is this: *They that are led by the Spirit of God are the sons of God* (Romans 8:14) also, *He will teach you all things* (1 John 2:27).

The process of events should never be the focus but the end of such events which always turn out glorious if we give time its full expression

CHAPTER 5

GOD'S RECIPE FOR CHANGE

Many times, people go through difficult times in their lives and they wonder where God is? They get mad that God is allowing them to go through tough times and is not helping them, yet God already told us in His word that He is with us and will never leave us nor forsake us.

Hebrews 13:5 (AMPC) says:

> *Let your character or moral disposition be free from love of money [including greed, avarice, lust, and craving for earthly possessions] and be satisfied with your present [circumstances and with what you have]; for He [God] Himself has said, I will not in any way fail you nor give you up nor leave you without support. [I will] not, [I will] not, [I will] not in any degree leave you helpless nor forsake nor let [you] down (relax My hold on you)! Assuredly not!*

Has He not said it, and will He not do it? All you must do is stay in His word *because God's word is His recipe for change.*

God always refers us to His word and the author of the scriptures which is the Holy Spirit. If you do not create time to study God's word and know it for yourself, then you will suffer for a long time.

Put His word first place and give it priority in your life. His word is His recipe for change. Let the word of God be the standard by which you live your everyday life. He said, *heaven and earth will pass away but my words shall not pass away* (Matthew 24:35). The Bible says, *forever thy word is settled in heaven* (Psalm 119:89).

All of heaven is at obeisance to His word. The word is functioning perfectly in heaven but that will not help you because we don't live in heaven; you have to bring the word into your life here on earth where you live. It is your responsibility to make the word of God work for you here on earth.

In Acts 20:32, Paul says:

> *And now, brethren, I commend you to God, and to the word of His grace, which is able to build you up, and to give you an inheritance among all them which are sanctified.*

Paul would not commend us to the word if it did not work in his life and if he did not taste the power thereof.

If you want to make changes in your life, then I commend you fully to God and to the word of His grace. His word is able to make you whatever you want to be and is able to build your life so beautifully well. All you need is in His word. His word is the answer!

A lasting change is change in the word and by the word

Let Him Help You

Jesus said in Mathew11:28,

> *Come unto me, all ye that labour and are heavy laden,*
> *and I will give you rest.*

Quit struggling and embrace the Holy Spirit. He will direct your path. He is always willing to help. He is the one who calls out to us. He called out to Adam in the garden when he sinned by eating the forbidden fruit, and still clothed him (Genesis 2:4, 3:24). His eyes are to and fro the earth looking for whom he may show Himself strong on their behalf (2 Chronicles 16:9).

God said in Isaiah 41:10,

> *Fear thou not; for I am with thee: be not dismayed; for*
> *I am thy God: I will strengthen thee; yea, I will help*
> *thee; yea, I will uphold thee with the right hand of my*
> *righteousness.*

Isaiah 41:13 says:

> *For I the* LORD *thy God will hold thy right hand, saying*
> *unto thee, Fear not; I will help thee.*

> **I will rather put one trust in God than a million**
> **in man**

God admonishes you in the above scriptures not to fear for He will help you. First, He lets you know that He is with you, so while you are thinking no one cares, He says to you, that He is with you and the result of being with you, is that He will help you.

The Bible says in Mathew 23:37,

> *O Jerusalem, Jerusalem, thou that killest the prophets, and stonest them which are sent unto thee, how often would I have gathered thy children together, even as a hen gathereth her chickens under her wings, and ye would not!*

Notice here that Jesus was willing and desiring to help bring them together like a hen gathers her brood, but the people were not. It's frustrating when you want to reach out to someone who is in dire need and yet the person is not allowing you. This statement doesn't seem like one which Jesus made smiling or rejoicing, but from a sincere desire and willingness to help Jerusalem. If only we would stop putting the blame on God when things go bad and receive His arm of love, friendship, and trust; we will not go through the difficulties we often find ourselves in.

God is more willing to help us than we could ever be willing to receive

He said in Isaiah 1:18,

> *Come now, and let us reason together, saith the LORD: though your sins be as scarlet, they shall be as white as snow; though they be red like crimson, they shall be as wool.*

Here is another invitation from God to mankind; such amazing love that the Father has bestowed on us, calling us affectionately and passionately so He could reason with us. How better can this get. If you are in a predicament and wondering why God is not helping you, my question to you is this? Why did He have to go through the trouble to send Jesus to die for us, and then not be ready to be with us in difficult times? That would be bad investment. He gave His son so that we may not only be cleansed from our sins but also to have life, the *Zoe* life, eternal life, a life beyond this world; that we might be in fellowship with Him and be one with Him. We cannot be one with Him and He folds His hands to watch us go through challenges without doing anything; far from it.

Always, the Lord invites us to allow Him to help us. He is our father; He created us and loves us so much (John 3:16). If He could give Jesus to us, how will He not with Jesus give us all things (Romans 8:32).

The Bible says it's the Father's good pleasure to give us the Kingdom (Luke 12:32). Be confident of His love for you and His desire to help you, at any time, at any point, and at every count.

Months ago, I had a friend who was about to give birth to her first baby, and I was so excited and ready to be there for her every step of the way. She promised to call me as soon as the bundle of joy arrived. However, days went by, but I received no call. Her husband later informed me that she had put to birth. I rang her line severally, sent messages; every effort to reach out to her proved abortive. I felt bad that she wouldn't let me help in whatever way I could and suddenly the Spirit of God whispered to me; He said, "this is exactly how I feel when you don't ask for my help". My goodness, I felt bad the more and apologised to the Holy Spirit promising to ask Him for help always.

How God wants us to always talk to Him. How He wishes we called Him when there was a challenge instead of looking for a friend to talk to. He is a friend who sticks closer than a brother and a very present help in times of need (Psalm 46:1).

> *The arm of flesh is designed to fail; why depend on the resource rather than the source?*

The Bible says in Exodus 11:7,

> *But against any of the children of Israel shall not a dog move His tongue, against man or beast: that ye may know how that the LORD doth put a difference between the Egyptians and Israel.*

God delivered the children of Israel with a mighty hand after 430 years of slavery in Egypt. He destroyed every first born in the land of Egypt from the first born of Pharaoh who sat on the throne to the first born of the female servant behind the hand mill (Exodus 11:4-6). The Israelites were untouched and preserved. Like Moses said, so that they might know that the Lord does make a difference between those who belong to Him and those who do not belong to Him. It is His greatest desire to help you. Only let Him do so.

> *How pleasing to know He distinguishes and separates us to Himself to pour out His love on us*

Change in the Word and by the Word

Hebrews 4:12 reads:

> *For the word of God is quick, and powerful, and sharper than any two-edged sword, piercing even to the dividing*

asunder of soul and spirit, and of the joints and marrow,
and is a discerner of the thoughts and intents of the heart.

The word is all knowing and knows exactly what you are going through. The word of God can divide between joints and marrows, and pierces even to the dividing asunder of the soul and spirit. The word of God knows where the pain is, what you feel in your body, and knows how to get it out. Go for the word today.

Jesus said in John 6:63,

It is the Spirit that quickens, the flesh profits nothing, the
words that I speak to you, they are Spirit and they are life.

The message translation says the Spirit can make life. Sheer muscle and will power do not make anything happen. Every word He speaks to us is a Spirit word and life making. The word "quicken" is a Greek word meaning to produce a life, to cause to live, to make alive, to give life, invigorate, restore to life, give increase to life. It is only the Spirit of God that can bring back old or dead dreams to life, make dead businesses come alive, bring back dead bodies alive, make dead relationships live, restore dead marriages etc.

I would not spend one moment looking for help when
I have the helper in me

When the Spirit of God is involved in anything, the necessary result or consequence is that He will quicken it by making it alive. Is your business falling apart? Have you tried all efforts to attract customers and make it thrive, but it seems the more efforts you put in, the more you fail? Fear not, I have good news for you; the Spirit of God is present even now as you read this book to give life to that business.

Perhaps it is your marriage; everyday gets worse than the previous, the arguments, quarrels and fights are beginning to get the children and neighbours attention, and this embarrasses you greatly. Maybe you cannot recall the last time you had a peaceful moment with your spouse and things are deteriorating; I say to you today, have no fear. It is never too late with God. Jesus appeared at Lazarus' house four days after Lazarus was dead. Everyone thought He was late including Martha, but Jesus told her; *"If you only believe you will see the power of God"* (John 11:40). I am also saying to you today, if you would only believe, you will see the power of God. Let the life giver restore your marriage and bring a whole new life and freshness to it or whatever it is that you may be dealing with.

Believe always gives birth to the miraculous

Someone reading this might say, "is it that easy"? "Just like that"? "Do you know what has gone wrong in the past"? Well it's not in my place to know what has been happening because that won't change a thing. However, I'm letting let you know that the monarch of the universe, the Father of Abraham, Isaac and Jacob, the one who brought the children of Israel out of Egypt with all the long years of suffering, the very Spirit that raised Jesus up from the dead, will give life to whatever is seemingly dead in your life or that of your loved ones. Put the word of God in your heart and allow it to gain the ascendancy over your mind, by meditating on it, and as you speak forth the word, it will produce the desired change.

Joshua 1:8 says:

> *This book of the law shall not depart from your mouth*
> *but you shall meditate in it day and night, that you may*

observe to do according to all that is written in it for then thou shalt make thy way prosperous, and then thou shalt have good success.

When you give attention to God's word, the word will make you a success. The word of God is your guarantee for success in life and for the change you require.

Jesus told the devil in Matthew 4:4, *man shall not live by bread alone, but by every word that proceeds from the mouth of God.* The word "every" signifies its importance, its totality and completeness; not some, not a little, but every word. Let your life rest completely on *every* word of God. Let it be your anchor, support, life, and everything.

Time after time, I heard Pastor Chris chorus that "one word from God can change your life forever". How true this is. That one word is coming to you right now. The word for the now, the rhema word, the word needed now for your challenge has come to you to effect that change. No wonder the psalmist said, thou hast exalted your word more than all your names (Psalm 138:2). The word of God has come to dwell in you richly as you study this book. Change has come.

I take responsibility for my success by using the power embedded in my words

The Holy Spirit is the Answer

Jesus said in John 14:16,

And I will pray the Father, and he shall give you another Comforter, that he may abide with you forever; Even the

Spirit of truth; whom the world cannot receive, because it seeth Him not, neither knoweth Him: but ye know Him; for he dwelleth with you, and shall be in you.

Firstly, the Spirit of God is with you even now to comfort you in whatever challenge you may be in. He doesn't just stop at comforting you, He is the Spirit of truth and you can trust that any direction or instruction He gives you is the truth. He has all the answers to help you make the necessary changes in your life. He brings to us the word of the father and teaches us His word. He will teach you the word of God to apply to your situation and cause a change no matter how bad the case is.

John 14:26 says:

But the Comforter, which is the Holy Ghost, whom the Father will send in my name, he shall teach you all things, and bring all things to your remembrance, whatsoever I have said unto you.

Also let's look at 1 John 2:27,

But the anointing which ye have received of Him abideth in you, and ye need not that any man teach you: but as the same anointing teacheth you of all things, and is truth, and is no lie, and even as it hath taught you, ye shall abide in Him.

Amazing scriptures! Even if I ended this book here, these verses are enough to bring about all the changes you desire to see in your life.

Abiding in Christ brings rest from troubles

The Holy Spirit is your helper, which we already talked about; reminding you again that you are not alone as you probably thought. He will teach you all things. My goodness! How blessed we are to have the person of the Holy Spirit, God Himself, living inside us and teaching us all things. In other words, whether it is in your field of expertise, He will teach you all things; be it in politics, in agriculture, in media and technology, in your family, in your health and your marriage, whatever and wherever the change is needed, He will teach you all things. Not some things, but ALL things!

Notice also that both scriptures talked about the same thing. About the Holy Ghost and how that He will teach you and bring to your remembrance all of God's word. Recall we discussed that God's recipe for change is His word; now, you have the Holy Ghost teaching you His word concerning that challenge which will bring about the change that you require. You can trust that all He teaches you is true and not a lie, for He is the Spirit of truth. However, there is an instruction which you are to follow in 1 John 2:27, *you are to abide, remain in Him*. When you do your part by abiding in Him, you can be certain that He will do His part in helping you come out of that predicament.

> *The power of both the written word and the living word makes change inevitable*

Power to Cause Changes

Every child of God is equipped with power and authority to effect any change they so desire in their lives.

Let us look at a few scriptures.

Acts 1:8 reads:

> *But ye shall receive power, after that the Holy Ghost is come upon you: and ye shall be witnesses unto me both in Jerusalem, and in all Judaea, and in Samaria, and unto the uttermost part of the earth.*

In the previous text, we just discussed about the Holy Spirit who is your helper and your teacher, who will teach you all things to enable you make a change in your circumstances. Here, you will learn about the authority and power you have to make changes when the Holy Ghost comes upon you and takes His abode in you. The power that you need all resides in the Holy Ghost. When He comes in to live in you, weakness is replaced with His power and that power causes you to go where you should go, say what you should say and change what you desire.

The Greek word for receive in Acts 1:8 is "*lambano*" which means to lay hold of or to lay claim.

How amazing it is to effect changes in our lives when we are equipped with the knowledge of God's word in all spiritual wisdom and understanding.

The next word to lay emphasis is "power" which means "*dunamis*" in the Greek translation. Dunamis is inherent power. Power for performing miracles, power residing in a thing by virtue of its nature.

So, let us read Acts 1:8 this way:

And you (put your name) shall "*lambano*" "*dunamis*"- "*ability*" to cause changes after the Holy Ghost is come upon you.

I can see someone "*lambano-ing*" your promotion and health right now. Glory to God. Go forth and lay a hold of what is yours. Take it. Do not negotiate, lay claim of it. Lay a hold of that good health. The devil may come with all kinds of attack on your body but shout out in the name of Jesus, "I refused to be sick anymore". I take a hold of my health because it is mine. Yes, it is yours. Jesus paid the full penalty for it and no sickness can ravage your body.

Can you see that change has come? Ensure that you do not negotiate with anything or anyone. Take what rightfully belongs to you. The victorious life in Christ is yours and nothing can stop that.

Power is made available in the work of witnessing

CHAPTER 6

THE PLACE OF PRAYER
IN CHANGE

T
here is nothing you cannot change when you pray, and the place of prayer cannot be over-emphasized.

The reason some people feel helpless when they go through difficult situations is because they do not pray. You must understand that prayer is very important and is a very necessary tool in causing changes in any aspect of your life.

It is time to start praying if you have not been doing so or stopped for whatever reason. As you continue in God's word, the Holy Spirit will guide you on how to pray.

Recall that I have shown you in the scriptures that the Holy Ghost gives you the power to make changes, and He is your teacher who will teach you all things. As you start out in prayer, He will give you directions on how you should study His Word and on what you should pray for.

Romans 8:26 (AMP) reads:

> In the same way the Spirit [comes to us and] helps us in
> our weakness. We do not know what prayer to offer or how
> to offer it as we should, but the Spirit Himself [knows our
> need and at the right time] intercedes on our behalf with
> sighs and groanings too deep for words.

There is no need to feel sorry for yourself when you are just a prayer
away to get your desired change.

Jude 1:20 (AMPC):

> But you, beloved, build yourselves up [founded] on your
> most holy faith, make progress, rise like an edifice higher
> and higher], praying in the Holy Spirit.

This is very instructive. Each time you pray (especially in the spirit), you
are being built up to your most holy faith. Your most holy faith is that
highest point of your faith when you know of a certainty that you have
the answer to whatever you prayed for; when that happens, you can be
sure to have made progress. Each time you pray in the spirit, you are
making progress and rising like an edifice. An edifice is a tall, great, and
imposing building. Whenever you pray, you are rising like that gigantic
building, higher and higher. Note that this experience is only felt when
you pray in the spirit which means to pray in other tongues.

**He called us to pray because He made every
arrangement to answer**

Apostle Jude by the inspiration of the Holy Ghost admonishes you,
calling you beloved, which means that you are worthy of love. This

should let you know that you are not alone in that challenge. You are not a "nobody", you are worthy of love; that is why Jesus paid for your sins. He says to you, build-up yourselves- do not just build around. Build your change on your most holy faith; rise as a large massive structure. When you pray in the Holy Ghost, there's one thing that is sure to happen to you; you will definitely rise from your present state to a higher, renewed, refreshed level or state as God intended for you.

Do not feel abandoned, condemning yourself for whatever predicament you are in. It makes no difference if you are the cause of your present state or not. The blood of Jesus already made provisions for all the mistakes you could ever make now and in the future. He settled it on the cross by dying for you.

If there is a man to call out in prayer, there is a God to reach out in answer

He said, "it is finished" meaning that the pain is finished, the sickness is finished etc. They are completely finished; nothing missing, nothing lacking; the evidence that it was totally finished was the resurrection. If Jesus did not finish defeating the devil, He would not have resurrected. The resurrection is proof positive that all you are going through is finished. Now what you need is to take advantage of the power of Jesus' resurrection and apply it in every area of your life, where you require a change. No demon hatched out of hell can stop that change. Remember, He is the Father of Spirits, without Him was not anything made that was made (John 1:3).

1 Corinthians 14:4 says:

> *He that speaketh in an unknown tongue edifieth Himself;*
> *but he that prophesieth edifieth the church.*

Jesus said in Mark 16:17,

> *And these signs shall follow them that believe, in my name,*
> *shall they cast out devils, they shall speak in new tongues.*

Speaking in tongues is for every Christian, and not a selected few, so start praying in the Holy Ghost and rise like an edifice; make progress, change that situation. As you pray, and it looks as though things are not changing, you can add fasting to it. Fasting and praying alongside helps to sharpen our spiritual antenna to hear clearly from God and receive the finest signals from the Spirit. It also enables us to give our undivided attention to study His word and receive directions from Him. Change is inevitable when we put these principles to work.

Change is inevitable in the place of prayer

James 5:16-17(AMPC):

Our emphasis is on the second sentence in verse 16:

> *The earnest (heartfelt, continued) prayer of a righteous*
> *man makes tremendous power available [dynamic in its*
> *working].*

> *Elijah was a human being with a nature such as we have*
> *[with feelings, affections, and a constitution like ours]; and*
> *he prayed earnestly for it not to rain, and no rain fell on*
> *the earth for three years and six months.*

1 Kings 18:42 reads:

> *So, Ahab went up to eat and to drink. And Elijah went up to the top of Carmel; and he cast Himself down upon the earth and put His face between His knees.*

Your prayer must be heartfelt, which means your emotions must be involved. It must be enough to get God's attention. If it gets your attention, then it will surely get God's attention and it must be continuous. Such prayers are always dynamic, effective, and produces result. This was how Elijah prayed.

The Bible says he prayed earnestly; that means in a serious manner, not lightly or casually. In the above scriptures, Ahab was asked by Elijah to go up and eat and drink while Elijah himself went up to the top of Mount Carmel to pray. The scriptures reveals the position Elijah took while praying for rain to fall; he bowed down on the ground and put His face between His knees.

I will continually give myself to prayer because in it I see solutions to life's challenges

For him to assume that position in prayer shows how earnest and intense that prayer must have been. That was not a casual prayer to be taken lightly else the Bible would not have said in James 5:17 that he prayed earnestly. This is to inspire faith in you to be earnest in your prayers when you want to effect changes in your life; like James, your rain of health, provisions or whatever you desire will pour out on you.

The prayer that works is the prayer that is heartfelt

Pray with Thanksgiving

Philippians 4:6-7 says:

> *Be careful about nothing but in everything by prayer and supplication with thanksgiving let your request be made known unto God, [7] and the peace of God which passeth all understanding shall keep your hearts and minds through Christ Jesus*

There is no point being troubled about your predicament or whatever you are going through. Worrying will not solve any problem; it would rather complicate it. Once you recognise that things are not going well the way it ought to, be determined and ready to cause a change by applying the principles enumerated in the above scripture.

The miracle of thanksgiving is like the miracle of the appearance of the sun and moon- constant and never failing

First, it says be *anxious* for nothing. Nothing changes when we get anxious, worried, or troubled. Second, it says for *nothing*; the challenge you are facing is nothing because God calls it nothing, even though it looks insurmountable.

The next principle is to pray and supplicate- supplication means seeking, making an entreaty to God, a petition, and a request.

The last principle is the principle of thanksgiving. Be thankful for the challenge and predicament you find yourself, be thankful that you have been able to recognise the need for a change, and for answers you have received when you pray.

Verse 7 in Philippians 4 tells us what will happen when we put these principles to work. It starts with a conjunction "and", connecting all that you have done in verse 6 with the resulting consequences in verse 7.

It reads: *And the peace of God which passeth all understanding shall keep your hearts and minds*

The resulting effect of not being anxious, praying, supplicating, and thanking God is the gift of peace amid storms. This peace exempts you from rage and havoc. It is a state of tranquillity. Peace comes with security and safety (from the pains or harm of whatever your present predicaments may have caused you).

The effects of peace and harmony produces safety and prosperity

The effect of peace also produces quietness and confident trust in God (Isaiah 32:17). It is God's desire that as you go through the storms of life, you can always have a peaceful disposition knowing that nothing can ever defeat you. He rightly said: *when you pass through the waters, He will be with you; And through the rivers, they shall not overflow you. When you walk through the fire, you shall not be burned, Nor shall the flame scorch you* (Isaiah 43:2).

God never leaves you in the dark when you go through challenges. He has given you His word to use for your benefit and to change any circumstance. His word is the manual for life, with principles to apply and get the results that you need. If you do not put these principles to work, you will live a life of struggles, and that is not what He wants for you.

Think about this, a manufacturer made a device and attached with it the manual for operating that device. If you refuse to use the manual, you will struggle with operating that device and you may use it ineffectively as was originally designed, and it may not serve its full purpose neither will you enjoy it completely.

It is the same thing with God's word. If you refuse to use the manual of God which is the word of God and the principles contained therein, you will live a life of struggles.

There is so much power in thanksgiving, so when you pray, do not forget to thank God for the prayers answered.

Jeremiah 30:19 reads:

> *And out of them shall proceed thanksgiving and the voice of them that make merry: And I will multiply them, and they shall not be few; I will also glorify them, they shall not be small.*

The scripture above outlines the importance of thanksgiving. Notice here that thanksgiving proceeded from them and as a result, God promised that He will multiply them and they won't be few; as if that wasn't enough, He also glorified them, so they won't be small.

The kingdom formula- thanksgiving and praise equals to abundance and plenty

The Hebrew word for multiply is *"rabbah"* which means to become great, become many, to grow great, to make large, enlarge and increase exceedingly. To glorify means to be rich, be glorious, and honourable.

This is so wonderful to see that all these great promises arose because of thanksgiving. This is one of the secrets of the power of thanksgiving; when you pray to God concerning any matter at all, you should do so in thanksgiving and you will certainly receive that which you asked of Him. Never under-estimate the place of prayer and thanksgiving in making a change. Go right ahead where you are and pray with thanksgiving, receiving your desired results. Amen!

Thanksgiving gives access to prepared miracles

Chapter 7

MAKE THE CHANGE

Au that you have learnt from the first chapter of this book till now, was for this moment. This is the moment for action. The time to take that deliberate and bold step. We are not mere talkers but also doers.

Let us look at some scriptures in the Bible which emphasizes doing God's word.

James 1:25 says:

> *But whoso looketh into the perfect law of liberty, and continueth therein, he being not a forgetful hearer, but a doer of the work, this man shall be blessed in His deed.*

If you do not "do" the word, you shall not be "BLESSED". It's only when the deed is done that the blessings come; it is the word of God that you do (practise).

The blessings follow a word-based action

2 Corinthians 3:18 reads:

But we all, with open face beholding as in a glass the glory of the Lord, are changed into the same image from glory to glory, even as by the Spirit of the Lord.

This verse is perfectly rendered. You have been beholding (looking, reading) God's word, which is His glory from the beginning of this book till now.

The first thing to note here as written by Paul is that anybody can become what God wants him or her to become. The ability is granted every single human being on the face of the earth. How do I know? Because the bible says we "ALL". Do not short-change yourself; do not think it is only a selected few that are meant to succeed. Do not label yourself as the unfortunate one, the one without connections, not educated enough, not wise enough, not strong enough, not rich enough; a thousand times No. Paul says we ALL, that means change for all; change for as many that will come boldly to the throne room of God to receive mercy and obtain favour in times of need.

Next, He says with open, unveiled face, beholding as in a glass the glory of the Lord. Beholding as in a glass means that the reflection of your face when you look into the mirror is exactly you. In other words, when you look at God's word which is His glory, you are changed, transformed, metamorphosed, transfigured into the exact image of God's word.

The mirror principle is becoming what you look at

If someone who is sick looks at Isaiah 53:5 which says, "by His stripes you are healed", several times a day, continuously, such a person will become what Isaiah said- healed. It makes no difference what the ailment is, what the doctor said or did not say; even though it is incurable (that's man's definition and limitation of knowledge not God's), diabetes, hypertension, HIV, cancer or any disease at all. As you look into the glory of the Lord, which is the word of God, you are inadvertently being *changed* into health that you see in the word, *even as by the Spirit of God.*

Isn't it wonderful that the change comes by the Spirit of God? This is a lasting change. A change not by drugs or medications but change by the Spirit of God who is the Spirit of life. So Amazing!

God says in Isaiah 43:19,

> *Behold, I will do a new thing; now it shall spring forth; shall ye not know it? I will even make a way in the wilderness, and rivers in the desert.*

This book is written solely for those who are tired of yesterday, tired of their past and their present circumstances and ready to embrace a new level. I implore you at this point to fix your gaze and attention intently on the change you are about to make, for the time to practically make that change is now.

Focusing on the new things brings more peace than gazing at the past where no change can be made

Recall I did mention the demand of honesty in previous chapters; now is the time to actualise it. To make a change, you must locate your present position in the change that you desire; perhaps it is in your health, finances, job, or business etc.

Secondly, you must see what the next level is going to be. How do you see? You see through your mind which is inundated by the word of God. You must be able to erase the previous ideas that are not in line with God's word.

For change to take place, it must first start from the mind

Change through the Mind

Romans 12:2 says:

And be not conformed to this world: but be ye transformed by the renewing of your mind, that ye may prove what is that good, and acceptable, and perfect, will of God.

How important this is. If only we put this truth to work, we will experience the miraculous in our lives through the power of our minds. Paul lets us know that God gave us our minds for our transformation. The Greek word is *"metamorphoo"* which means to transform, transfigure, to change into another form, to metamorphose.

The human mind can create anything you desire. Its potentials and possibilities are limitless. You can influence the way you think to become more successful. It will interest you to know that you are what you think (Proverbs 23:7). The present state you are in is because of your thoughts, and your next level will also be greatly determined by your thoughts. This is why the scripture above admonishes you to be transformed by the renewing of your minds.

Your life and your personality are the expressions of your mind; how you live, the way you talk or behave, your attitude and choice of words, are all the outward expressions of your mind. If you require a change in your life, then you need to work on your mind and the thoughts you allow into it. Change the contents of your mind with the word of God, and the results will show both in your character and way of life.

Understand your Mind

Make a well determined effort to control the thoughts that goes through your mind. You cannot expect to be rich when all you think and brood about is failure and creating pictures of failure in your mind; those pictures have been registered in your mind and ultimately produced the failure that you experience. This is the reason why you go for a job interview and you are not chosen, you write an exam and fail despite your hard work in studying, you write a proposal which looks perfect by all standards yet it's rejected, you began a relationship that looked promising and when you should have taken it to the next level, it crumbles. It is not because anyone is against you rather; it's primarily because you have not managed your mind properly to delete those pictures of failures and defeat and to replace them with thoughts of success, progress and increase.

The mind is too important to be ignored. When you understand and learn how to manage your mind, you will upgrade your level and enlarge your estate. Consciously erase all thoughts and pictures of the past failures, disappointments, sickness, and replace them with the right thoughts of peace, success etc.

The pain of the past blinds the glory of the present and future

Hebrews 4:12 says:

> *The word of God is quick and powerful and sharper than any two-edged sword piercing even to the dividing asunder of soul and spirit who on of the joints and marrow and is a discerner of the thoughts an intent of the Heart.*

The mind is the seat of man's reasoning and thoughts. It has the power to imagine and recognise. It is responsible for processing your feelings and emotions which eventually leads to your character and actions.

An important word in the scripture above is "***thought***" and it means to create, to process, to reason, to collect, to design or purpose.

This means that you can create, recall, process and imagine something. Hence you can create your change, create the life you desire; imagine and process the images in your mind and give them the positive meaning. When you look at an image, for example a ball, whatever you interpret the image to be is registered in your mind: if your mind can't interpret it, then it'll make no sense to you.

2 Corinthians 4:16 reads:

> *For this cause, we faint not but though our outward man perish, yet the inner man is renewed day by day.*

Paul lets us know that we have an outward man and an inner man. The outward man is our conscious mind which relates with our physical body and its five senses (the sense of sight, hearing, smell, touch, and taste). The human mind receives information from its environment through its five senses. The inward man is the human spirit and his soul. Your soul is your mind, which sits your will, emotions, reasoning, and intellect. Every human being has a spirit and a soul. It is the spirit that receives the salvation of Jesus Christ. Your mind connects your body to your spirit.

Now that you understand how important the mind is, you must educate it by renewing your mind. Educate your mind with the right words, right thoughts, right pictures, and the right imaginations. Consciously have pictures of positivity, success, and increase. If you require a change in your finances, perhaps you are in debt and unable to afford the necessary things of life, you must renew the way you think about your financial situation. See yourself having a good business and increasing your finances enough to pay your debts and so much more. Imagine yourself being rich and staying rich. Create the images of financial success in your thoughts and it will register in your mind. Stay on it. Do not change those thoughts or images you have created. Keep them in your mind until there is a change.

The word of God is the material with which you use to renew your mind

It's Time to Create

Just in case you thought you are the only one who is in a difficult situation, you will be amazed to know that God Himself had a challenge and He made a change.

Follow me on this expose and let us see what God did.

Genesis 1:1-5:

> *In the beginning God **created** the heaven and the earth.*
>
> *And **the earth was without form, and void**; and darkness was upon the face of the deep. And the **Spirit of God moved upon the face of the waters.***
>
> *And God **said**, let there be light: and **there was light.***
>
> *And God **saw** the light, that it was **good**: and God divided the light from the darkness.*
>
> *And God **called** the light Day, and the darkness he called Night. And the evening and the morning were the first day.*

The first person who ever made a change in His situation was God. The Bible records in Genesis chapter one that in the very beginning, God created the heavens and the earth but between verse one and two of the same chapter, something happened, and its account is given in Jeremiah 4:23-26.

It reads:

> *I beheld the earth, and, lo, it was without form, and void; and the heavens, and they had no light.*
>
> *I beheld the mountains, and, lo, they trembled, and all the hills moved lightly.*
>
> *I beheld, and, lo, there was no man, and all the birds of the heavens were fled.*

*I beheld, and, lo, the fruitful place was a wilderness, and
all the cities thereof were broken down at the presence of
the LORD, and by His fierce anger.*

God had a challenge after creating the heavens and the earth, and He
knew He needed to fix it. He knew He needed to make a change. He
did not whine, regret, or feel bad. He did not think that was the end. He
knew exactly what to do and so immediately, the Spirit of God hovered
over the face of the waters. Notice that the first thing God did was a
decision to create the change and the next thing He did was to swing
into action as the Holy Ghost hovered upon the face of the waters.

The Hebrew word for "without form" means confusion, emptiness,
chaos. Is that your situation right now? Be patient to read what God did
in His case so you know exactly how to apply the principles.

The Spirit of God hovered upon the face of the waters which means
to brood, to move. To brood means He was walking on the situation,
moving on it, and releasing His power for the change that was to occur.

**I would rather create a new thing than try to mend
a shattered past**

Job 26:13 says, *by His breath the skies became fair.*

Immediately after the Spirit moved over the face of the waters, God said
"let there be light". Remember the earth was full of darkness, confusion,
and chaos; God said exactly what He wanted to see which was light and
the bible says there was light; not there will be light but there was light.

Speak Forth

The next thing He did was to *"speak"*. All this process of creation took place in the realm of the Spirit, as you study the account in Genesis chapters one and two.

God never spoke out His disappointment or regrets but spoke what He wanted to see. Do not speak your fears, anger, disappointment, and complaints; that will never work. Speak what you want to create which is the change. After doing that, you must *"see it"*. To speak means to declare, to certify, to command. As you get ready to speak change, remember that you are certifying new things into existence.

I see when I speak, and I speak what I see

See

The next word I like us to look closely at here is the word *"see"*: derived from the Hebrew word *"raah"* which means to perceive, to regard, to observe, to find out, to discern. The essence of seeing is to find out if you like the picture of the change you are creating, if it's complete or if there's something else you would like to add or subtract before the final picture is fixed in your mind. Remember, as a man thinketh in his heart, so is he (Proverbs 23:7), so you will be the exact picture that you create in your mind.

In verse 4, God saw that the light was good. You need to see that your creation is good, else you create something that is bad. The reason people live the wrong lives and get into all kinds of trouble is because they are busy creating the wrong pictures in their minds: pictures of negativity, fear, pain, etc. It is important to guard your heart because out of it are the issues of life. When creating a change, do it perfectly just as your heavenly Father is perfect (Mathew 5:48). You must ensure that your creation is good for God and for mankind, therefore it will be required of you to "see" your creation and be sure that it is good.

In the later part of verse 4, God divided the light from the darkness. It was important for Him to divide the past from the present, the darkness from the new light He created. Learn to separate your past from your present. You cannot change your past, but you can decide what happens in your present and your future.

Mark 2:21 (NIV) says:

> *No one sews a patch of unshrunk cloth on an old garment, otherwise, the new piece will pull away from the old making the tear worse.*

When you create a new picture and include the past failures in it, according to the bible, the present situation will be worse than the former.

The word enables me to see the unseen and bring it into existence

Call Forth

The next thing in creating is to "*call forth*". It means to recite, to proclaim, to read aloud, to preach, to name. This is akin to meditation. When God changed Abraham's name from Abram to Abraham in Genesis 17:5, Abraham believed it, saw himself as a father of many nations even when he had no son yet.

91

He began to recite it and called himself "the father of many nations" and it became exactly what he said.

Bless Your Creation

In verse 22 of the same chapter, God blessed everything He created, He saw that everything He created was good; He blessed them and commanded them to be fruitful and to multiply.

After seeing the job that you have created in your mind, have you considered if it's good? Does it look worthy of your status in Christ? Will it give you time to serve God? Is it the kind of job that will enable you to bless others? Will you preach the gospel to your co-workers? Can you see your next level? Now after seeing all these and you are certain that it is good, proceed to call it forth and pronounce your blessings on it. Tell your job to be fruitful and multiply, tell your job to create other branches and outlets for service to God and humanity and have what you say (Mark 11:23-24).

What I bless becomes fruitful but what I neglect becomes fruitless; I chose to bless my creations

CHAPTER 8

BECOME THE CHANGE

In the previous chapter we saw that God was also in a challenge and He made the change by applying the aforementioned principles. We saw that God spoke what He wanted to see, which was light. He saw that it was good including every other thing He created, He divided the darkness from the light, He called them forth and finally blessed them. He had a purpose for His creation, He told man to be fruitful and to multiply. How amazing to know that you can change anything you want to change and be anything you want to be, just like your God.

After the creation of man, which was in the spiritual realm, God formed man of the dust of the ground (Genesis 2:7). In the same vein, after you have created your change in the spirit realm, bring your creation into physical existence.

Every change is possible and guided by principles

The way to bring your change into the physical is through meditation and declaration of your new level and change.

The Bible says in Joshua 1:8 (AMPC):

> *This Book of the Law shall not depart out of your mouth,*
> *but you shall meditate on it day and night, that you may*
> *observe and do according to all that is written in it. For*
> *then you shall make your way prosperous, and then you*
> *shall deal wisely and have good success.*

The word meditate is from the Hebrew word "*hagah*" and it means to muse, to devise, imagine, moan, growl, utter and groan.

Meditation drives the word of God deep into your spirit until you become one with the word you meditate on. As you fix your mind on the change that you have created in the spirit realm, mediate on it continuously and before long, you will become what you meditated upon. It says the book of the law which is the word of God must not depart from your mouth. It did not say it shall not depart from your "mind" but from your "mouth". It means after creating your change in the spirit of your mind, you have to speak it forth, mutter it, growl and groan it, until it completely takes over your thoughts, your actions and your communications.

Notice that you are the one to make your way **prosperous**. Meditation makes your way prosperous because the more of the word you think on and talk, you will automatically act on what you think and say, and the result will be a prosperous way, a prosperous change.

Meditation guarantees you of not only success but good success

1 Timothy 4:15 says:

> *Meditate upon these things; give thyself wholly to them;*
> *that thy profiting may appear to all.*

Again, Paul admonishes us to meditate on the word, emphasizing on its importance; making sure to give thyself wholly, completely, solely to the word. The result of giving yourself wholly to meditating on His word is that your profiting, your change, your new level will appear to all. In other words, your profiting will be apparent, manifested, and evident to all. This lets you know that the change you produce through meditation will appear in the *physical* for all to see. Glory to God! *This is the way to become your change.*

You become your change through meditation

Change the Materials

While living in your change, it is important that you must not go back to the old life that put you in the previous mess. You must consciously change the books you were reading previously that made you think negatively, the news you listened to constantly that told nothing but fears and pessimism, you must change the friends you once kept who made you do things that were wrong (1Corinthians 15:33), and of course you must consistently renew your mind with God's word.

Be Bold and Courageous

God told Joshua time and again in Joshua 1:8,

> *Have not I commanded thee? Be strong and of a good courage; be not afraid, neither be thou dismayed: for the Lord thy God is with thee whithersoever thou goest.*

How important this is in becoming the change that you have created. There will be many things that will try to take you back to your past challenges but it's important to maintain your focus by being courageous. The devil may try to accuse you or bring thoughts of fear and defeat to you, but you must maintain your course and your confession of the "new you". The devil is called the accuser of the brethren (Revelation 12:10); resist him strongly and stay focused and courageous. When you resist the devil, he will certainly flee (James 4:7).

In John 8:10,

> *When Jesus had lifted up Himself, and saw none but the woman, he said unto her, Woman, where are those thine accusers? hath no man condemned thee?*

This is a case of the adulterous woman who was accused of adultery by the scribes and Pharisees and was brought to Jesus but the Master was wiser than them and caught them in their craftiness for they brought the woman to Him to tempt and to accuse Him. You must be ready to give bold answers to your accusers and detractors who may try to mock or tempt you.

> ***Your detractors only leverage on the opportunity you give them, when you resist them, they quit***

Keep talking your change. Do not stop for a second and do not waver. It is important to know that words are things, they are potent and have divine energy to produce exactly what you say. When you keep speaking forth your change, you are releasing power to the direction of your change; so stay your course, enjoy your new level, for God has given you all things to enjoy (1 Timothy 6:17).

Congratulations on making that change that you so desired!

Congratulations on your new level!

Congratulations on becoming your change!

Prayer of Salvation

I trust that you have been blessed by this book. The change that you desire is possible only in Christ, and if you have not given your life to Jesus Christ, I invite you to make Jesus Christ the Lord of your life today by praying this prayer:

"Dear Father, I believe with my heart that Jesus is the Son of the Living God. I believe that Jesus died for me and that God raised Him from the dead. I believe that He is alive today. I confess with my mouth that Jesus Christ is Lord. I confess that He is the Lord of my life from today. I am now born again. Thank you, Jesus, for saving my soul. Glory to God".

Congratulations, you are now a child of God.

HALLELUJAH!!!

To receive more information on how you can grow in your Christian faith, please contact us through any of the following contacts below:

AUSTRALIA   NIGERIA

+61449787446   +2348105833739
+61449066926

E-mail: makethechange58@gmail.com

everydaywithJesus2020@gmail.com

Imaobong Odutola, MD

Social Media Platforms:

Youtube: EVERY DAY WITH JESUS

Instagram: everydaywithjesus1

Facebook: EVERY DAY WITH JESUS

About the Author

Dr. Imaobong is a trained Medical Doctor and a Minister of the gospel who has ardently followed Jesus Christ since her high school days and preaching the gospel since 1998; having begun preaching to her friends, families, school mates, colleagues in Africa, Caribbean and now to the world at large.

She is the founder of *"Every day with Jesus"*, an Inspirational, Motivational, and Transformational program which teaches God's word daily on all the social media platforms.

Her love for the gospel of Jesus has brought several young people to Christ; being blessed by her messages through several outreaches and platforms over the years.

She is passionate about reaching the peoples of the world with the love of Christ contained in His word, in the demonstration of His Spirit and power. She seeks to help people discover and fulfil their purpose in Christ.

Dr. Imaobong and her husband, Dr. Michael who is also a Minister of the gospel are blessed with three lovely children.

Other Books by the Author

Make the Change Confession for Children

Make the Change Affirmation for Teenagers and Adults

Make the Change Divine Health Confessions

Make the Change Affirmations for Conception and Pregnancy

Hardened to Difficulties

References

The Strong's Bible and Concordance

V.E. Vine's Dictionary

All scripture quotations are taken from the King James Version of the Bible unless otherwise indicated